C
797.122 BAS
Bass, Scott.
Kayaking /
blk 1068927498

WITHDRAWN
WORN SOILED OBSOLETE

I0602376

KIDS' GUIDES

KAYAKING

by Scott Bass

Content Adviser: Robin Stanton,
Managing Editor, Canoe and Kayak
Magazine, Kirkland, Washington

The Child's World®

Published in the United States of America by The Child's World®
PO Box 326 • Chanhassen, MN 55317-0326 • 800-599-READ • www.childsworld.com

Acknowledgments

The Child's World®: Mary Berendes, Publishing Director

Editorial Directions, Inc.: E. Russell Primm, Editorial Director; Melissa McDaniel, Line Editor; Matt Messbarger, Project Editor and Editorial Assistant; Susan Hindman, Copy Editor; Susan Ashley, Proofreader; Terry Johnson, Olivia Nellums, Katharine Trickle, and Julie Zaveloff, Fact Checkers; Tim Griffin/IndexServ, Indexer; James Buckley Jr. and James Gigliotti, Photo Researchers and Selectors

Editorial and photo research services provided by Shoreline Publishing Group LLC, Santa Barbara, California

The Design Lab: Kathleen Petelinsek, Art Direction and Design; Kari Thornborough, Art Production

Photos

Cover: Charlie Munsey/Corbis; AFP/Corbis: 27; Ariel Skelley/Corbis: 18; Charlie Munsey/Corbis: 28; Corbis: 16; Douglas Peebles/Corbis: 11; Getty Images: 8, 19, 25; Joel W. Rogers/Corbis: 21; Marc Muench/Corbis: 22; Paul A. Souders/Corbis: 6, 12; Reuters NewMedia Inc./Corbis: 24; R.W. Jones/Corbis: 5; Tom Stewart/Corbis: 14; Wally McNamee/Corbis: 26.

Registration

Copyright © 2005 by The Child's World®. All rights reserved.
No part of this book may be reproduced or utilized in any form or by any means without written permission from the publisher.

Library of Congress Cataloging-in-Publication Data

Bass, Scott.
  Kayaking / by Scott Bass.
    v. cm. — (Kids' guides)
  Includes bibliographical references and index.
  Contents: Climb in a kayak—Gear and events—Kayaks in action—Kayaking stars and competition.
  ISBN 1-59296-208-4 (library bound : alk. paper) 1. Kayaking—Juvenile literature. [1. Kayaks and kayaking.] I. Title. II. Series. III. Kids' guides.
  GV784.3.B37 2005
  797.122'4—dc22   2003027372

CONTENTS

THE FREEDOM OF KAYAKING

Imagine yourself wedged into a

plastic boat roaring past huge boulders on a raging river. You dash down the river using the force of the whitewater waves to move to and fro. The sound of the crashing water is deafening. The wind stings your cheeks. The icy cold water numbs your fingers. You approach a 100-foot (30.5-meter) **chute** and propel yourself downward with a frenzy of paddling.

Kayaking is extreme, and not just in the X Games way. Actually, zooming through wild rapids in a plastic boat is more than extreme—some would say it is downright crazy. But kayaking offers a broad range of experiences, and they're not all about plunging over waterfalls.

For instance, imagine yourself paddling down a calm, crystal-clear river. Birds soar overhead. Large, puffy, white clouds drift through the blue sky. You hear the gentle lap of water against your boat's **hull.** It is just you, your kayak, and the peaceful surroundings of Mother Nature.

Kayaking offers extremely different experiences because it includes two completely different styles: touring (including sea touring) and whitewater. Touring kayaks are long and sleek and used in relatively calm water or in the ocean's currents. Whitewater kayaks are short and **blunt.** They're

If adventure is what you're looking for, kayaking can be a wild ride.

designed for flying down river rapids. One type of kayaking can be extremely peaceful; the other, extremely wild.

No matter which kayak style you choose (and you should try both), you will enjoy freedom. The beauty of kayaking is that water is no longer out of bounds. Using a kayak, you can explore Mother Nature's highways. A river or lake can take you to places you've never been and would have never gone. The kayaking experience is different each and every time. One day you may watch a pod of killer whales leap out of the water. The next day you may witness a flock of herons glide above the reeds of a lagoon. Mother Nature will invite you to her party. Adventure will be your host.

Paddling down a river is mentally rewarding. This is why kayaking is so popular. You can feel the power of the current and wind as you glide your boat along a riverbank. You can jolt your senses with the rush of riding white-water waves down a wild river. On top of that, it is a good form of exercise. And you can experience all this after taking the necessary lessons.

Oh, yeah—it's great fun, too!

This book examines kayaking history and kayaking gear. You'll get some basic instruction and meet the heroes of competitive kayaking. Then maybe your curiosity will be sparked and your appetite for adventure moistened. It will be time for you to get into a kayak—and into a whole new world.

Kayaking can offer a serene way to view nature's treasures.

CHAPTER one

CLIMB IN A KAYAK

Canoes, in one form or another, have
been around for 30,000 years. Researchers believe that the
Inuit built kayaks, which are simply enclosed canoes, as far
back as 10,000 years ago. The Inuit stretched animal skins
over frames built of driftwood and whale bones. The shelter
provided by the enclosed kayaks allowed them to remain
warm and comfortable while hunting. The word *kayak* means
"hunter's boat."

Explorers in Canada and Alaska saw Inuit using kayaks
as early as the 16th century. In 1866, John MacGregor, a young
British explorer, founded the Royal Canoe Club in England.
MacGregor is famous for being the first to tour the rivers of
Europe using his own Inuit-style kayak. MacGregor's club held
lively kayak races. Soon, kayak racing and touring found its way
back to North America, and a new sport was born.

Kayaking as a competitive sport took off when it was
accepted along with canoeing into the 1936 Olympic Games.
Originally, Olympic kayaking consisted of four events, the single
and pairs 1,000-meter and 10,000-meter races. Later, the whitewater race and **slalom** events were added.

Besides the two different styles of kayaking (touring and
whitewater), there are also two basic categories of kayaking:

Kayaking pros can do cool stunts even with older white-water kayaks such as this one.

competitive and recreational. Competitive kayaking involves

straight-line racing, along with whitewater challenges such as

freestyle or whitewater slalom. In freestyle competition, the kayaker performs particularly difficult or tricky **maneuvers.** Officials then judge the performance. The slalom competition is like downhill slalom skiing. Gates or poles are set up, and the kayakers are timed as they make their way around the gates.

Recreational kayaking includes open ocean touring, whitewater running, or lake touring. The vast majority of kayakers find plenty of excitement, exercise, and adventure in recreational kayaking. Whether we know it or not, getting in a boat and exploring is a part of our national identity. One simple forward stroke and we launch ourselves into the world of Lewis and Clark, Daniel Boone, or Huck Finn. And that points to the number-one reason that kayaking is such a popular and growing sport: both beginners and experts can do it and have a lot of fun. The kayaking experience is for everybody. It is unique, it is **accessible,** and it is inspiring.

BOOMING ON THE WATER!

Kayaking is a very fast-growing sport. According to one survey, in 2002 more than 10 million people in the United States went kayaking at least once. That is almost 1.5 million people more than had gone in 2001.

The survey also said that more than 2.2 million people go kayaking on a regular basis. We hope they all don't try to go on the same river at the same time!

CHAPTER two

GEAR AND EVENTS

There are about as many types of kayaks

as there are bicycles or snowboards. If you were buying a bike for road racing, you wouldn't pick a BMX or other dirt bike. And you wouldn't select a downhill snowboard if you were aiming to catch big air in a half-pipe. Which kayak is best suited for you depends partially upon your skill level. Longer, narrower kayaks aren't as stable or as user-friendly as shorter, wider kayaks. Luckily, kayaking is a family sport, so there are plenty of kid-sized kayaks available.

The other key factor to think about when choosing a kayak is what kind of water you will be on. Different kayaks work better in oceans, rivers, and whitewater. Here is a brief look at the types of kayaks:

Recreational Kayaks

These kayaks are perfect for still-water lake cruising, nature watching, or just leisurely paddling. They're generally shorter than other kayaks (9 to 15 feet [3 to 5 m] long) and are very stable. If you're looking for a simple means to get from point A to point B, then the recreational kayaks are for you. They don't have a storage hatch, so you can't go on long trips, but they are ideal for beginner paddlers. Recreational kayaks are a great start for your new life as a paddling adventurer. Most places that rent kayaks stock recreational kayaks for just that purpose—to get you on the water.

Touring Kayaks

These are stable, sturdy vessels with a closed hatch for stowing food and equipment. Touring kayaks (such as sea kayaks) can range from a narrow 20 inches (51 centimeters) to a very stable 25 inches (64cm) at the **beam.** Their width makes them stable. They are also longer by a few feet than recreational kayaks. Some touring kayaks tend to tip more, but after an hour or so (not to mention a few spills into the water), you'll get the hang of it. If you want to get a little closer to the action of the rough water, take in the scenery, and get a good workout, these cruisers are the SUVs of the kayak world.

Choose your destination or purpose, and then choose your type of kayak.

Racing Kayaks

These streamlined kayaks are fast and graceful. Their very narrow beam—often less than 20 inches (51 cm)—makes racing kayaks quite tippy. These are the kayaks that you'll see used in the sprint competition during the Olympic Games. Other

Racing kayaks are sleek and streamlined.

similar racing kayaks are used in the slalom events. These boats are built specifically for flat, calm water.

Whitewater Kayaks

These are the boats that put the X in extreme. Whitewater kayaks—bearing brand names such as Dagger and Riot—are designed specifically for rough-water or swift-flowing rivers. Their wide, flat hulls make them stable in **turbulent** river rapids. Squirt boats are one kind of kayak specially made for awesome stunt maneuvers. You'll need proper training, but there are some great kids' camps out there for those of you looking to get radical.

Other Kayaking Gear

You won't get anywhere with just a kayak. To actually get out on the water, you need other gear, too. Kayaking offers a boat-load (pardon the pun) of equipment and garb. Paddles, navigational tools, and clothing all play a part.

Like kayaks themselves, there are lots of different paddles to choose from. But kayakers really need to keep

> ## PARTS OF A KAYAK
> Bow: the front of the kayak (the nose).
> Stern: the back of the kayak.
> Cockpit: where you sit.
> Hull: the main body of the kayak (the bottom half).
> Deck: the top half of the kayak.
> Beam: the widest point of the kayak.

A knowledgeable kayak outfitter can supply you with a proper paddle and other equipment.

just two things in mind when choosing a paddle: length and material.

How long a paddle you need generally depends upon your height and the type of kayak you choose. If you go out on the water with the wrong paddle size, your stroke will feel awkward—kind of like blowing a bubble into the wind.

It won't be too much fun. Have yourself measured for the proper paddle at a kayak outfitter.

In the past, all paddles were made of wood. With today's technology, paddles are now made of materials that are lighter and stronger. Wood paddles are often the nicest to look at, but carbon fibers make new paddles featherlight and strong. Often, paddle makers will combine wood and carbon fiber. Fiberglass paddles are a great option as well. They are generally lighter than wood but cheaper than carbon fiber.

Along with the kayak and the paddle, another very important piece of gear you will need is the personal flotation device, or PFD. A life jacket of sorts, a PFD has a more comfortable, snug fit. You simply strap the PFD around your chest as you would a coat or jacket. **Do not ever get into any boat without a PFD securely strapped around your body.** The first rule of kayaking is to have fun, and you can't have fun if you are not safe. Plus, PFDs add another layer of warmth. Be sure to wear a helmet as well.

If you live in an area that is cool or even cold, or if the water temperature is cold, you'll need outerwear. Neoprene is a material used to make wet suits, and many kayakers wear a neoprene wet suit when in open water. Snug-fitting neoprene wet suits let a little bit of water in between your body and the wet suit. Your body then heats that thin layer of water up to body temperature, keeping you comfortable. Neoprene wet suits come in a variety of styles—from a full-length wet suit, which covers your entire body, to a simple vest or jacket.

This kayaker is prepared for rough waters.

Perhaps the hardest parts of your body to keep warm are your extremities—your fingers and toes. Booties, also made of neoprene rubber, warm your toes and feet. Pogies are fingerless mittens created specifically for the paddler. They allow your fingers to wrap around the paddle while keeping the wind and water off your hands. Booties and pogies are both very important if you plan on paddling in cooler climates.

Other gear to consider, depending on the difficulty or length of your trip, may include:

• A water-repellent jacket or pullover.

- A spray skirt. This fits tightly around your waist and over the opening of your kayak's cockpit. The skirt acts as a barrier between your lower half and the water. The skirt snaps on or can be attached with Velcro.

- A dry bag. Keep a change of clothes in this bag in case you get wet.

- An air horn or whistle. A noisemaking device could be used in case of emergency.

- A towrope. This comes in handy if you (or someone else) need help.

- Drinking water/snack.

- Compass.

- Sunscreen, sunglasses, and a hat.

JUST FOR KIDS

Although they haven't created a waterproof Xbox yet, kayak outfitters do make equipment with kids in mind. That equipment includes properly sized helmets and paddle shoes, snug-fitting PFDs, and sunglasses.

The Hobie Lanai is one of many great kayaks built specifically for kids. This kayak is only 9 feet [3 m] long, it is relatively lightweight [40 pounds [18 kilograms]], and, perhaps most important, it is very stable. The Hobie Lanai also boasts a built-in drink holder and plenty of storage space. Check it out at *www.hobiekayak.com.*

CHAPTER three

KAYAKS IN ACTION

The only real way to learn kayaking is

through some good instruction at a YMCA or a kayak camp or club. But here are some pointers that will give you a head start.

Getting In

Getting in and out of a kayak is no small feat. Kayaks are unstable when they are not moving. Getting in with someone to help you is easiest. Have the person hold your kayak to keep it steady and just step in and sit down. Other good ways to get into your kayak include when you're next to a dock or when you're in water you can stand up in.

Don't rock the boat! With a little instruction, kids can have fun on the water.

To move forward, rotate your shoulder and dig your paddle into the surface.

Once you're in the kayak, you'll need to **stabilize** yourself. You do this by using your paddle as a stabilizer—either against a dock or, if you're in shallow water, against the bottom of the lake. You'll also need to learn the bracing stroke. Bracing yourself with your paddle when you're not moving is something you will be doing a lot. The bracing stroke involves extending the flat side of your paddle against the surface of the water.

The Forward Stroke

To begin moving, use the forward stroke. The most important part of the forward stroke is shoulder rotation. Instead of reaching out in front of you with the paddle, first rotate your shoulder forward, and then dig your paddle into the water. Also, think about paddling as pulling yourself toward the paddle instead of pulling the paddle toward you.

When you take kayaking lessons, you'll learn other important techniques, including the sweep stroke (for turning), the draw stroke (for moving sideways), and going in reverse. But the forward stroke is the one you'll use most often. Remember to rotate before you reach.

Getting Out

Any water surface can switch from glassy to choppy in a matter of minutes. You'll need to learn the various bracing techniques to deal with such change. The forward stroke will get you to the rough water; the bracing stroke will help you handle it with confidence.

At some point, however, you and your kayak will get **capsized.** Remember, sitting in your kayak you're probably covered by a spray skirt. When you capsize, you're suddenly hanging upside-down in the water. You have to change that point of view right away!

You have two options. The first option is a "wet exit," which means you leave the kayak while underwater. The other option is called the Eskimo roll. An Eskimo roll is not some sort of whale-blubber sushi. Instead, it is the most efficient way to

turn your kayak back over without using a wet exit. The Eskimo

roll involves a series of body movements and paddling tech-

niques to turn your kayak 180 degrees. It takes some practice,

but when performed properly, the Eskimo roll is a smooth and

seamless maneuver.

Here's a man who has learned the Eskimo roll to turn right side up.

Kayaking can take you to some of the most beautiful places on Earth.

If you're interested only in recreational kayaking, the odds are you won't need to know how to perform an Eskimo roll. But if you take a touring or whitewater class, you'll probably be able to learn how to roll in about an hour. It's an awesome skill to have and will increase your paddling fun.

Planning Your Trek

You're all geared up and have had some lessons. Now comes the really fun part—going on a kayak trek. Hey, that's the beauty of kayaking: you get in the boat and go!

Whether your journey will be 10 yards (9 m) or 10 miles (16 kilometers), safety is always the number-one concern. You should check the weather forecast, put on a PFD, and tell someone where you are going. Always go kayaking with a buddy, in case of trouble. Going with a buddy makes it more fun, too!

If you're feeling adventurous, planning the trip is always lots of fun. There are few things more exciting than laying out a large, detailed map of rivers and waterways and choosing a route. The route you select will determine many things, including navigation, weather, food, equipment, and emergency needs. Plan smart. And remember: kayaking is an adventure. Explore. Search. Discover.

GET WET

As you plunge into the world of kayaking, you may notice that most kayakers are obsessed with the ideal of staying dry. Everything about kayaking gear, from the spray skirt to the outerwear, is centered on staying dry.

If you're properly outfitted (wet suit, outerwear, booties), getting wet shouldn't be an issue. So don't worry about it. You are in a water environment. Water is wet. You will get wet if you are in the water. Just let it happen—it's not a bad thing.

CHAPTER four

KAYAKING STARS

Just as there are street competitions

and vert competitions in skateboarding, there are also different types of kayak competitions. The two major areas of competition are flatwater and whitewater.

In flatwater sprint racing, kayakers use long, speedy kayaks and compete head-to-head on calm water for distances of 1,000 meters to 10,000 meters. Flatwater is a contest of

These flatwater racers made a big splash at the Olympic complex in Athens, Greece.

One thing is for sure in whitewater or freestyle kayaking: you're going to get wet!

speed, strength, and endurance in which athletes must use smooth paddling techniques. The Olympic program includes 12 sprint events.

Whitewater slalom competition consists of a 25-gate whitewater rapids course. Paddlers attempt to go through a series of upstream and downstream gates as quickly as possible without touching the slalom poles or missing slalom gates. The slalom courses are up to 600 meters long.

Wildwater competition combines the excitement of whitewater slalom with the strategy of a distance event. The racer's goal is to find the fastest of a series of lines through whitewater rapids. Theoretically, there is a narrow ribbon of whitewater that is faster than any other part of the river. The objective of the wildwater competition is to read the **eddies** and currents, find that ribbon, and advance the kayak as fast as possible.

In rodeo (or freestyle) kayaking, paddlers drop into a **hole** and then perform extreme maneuvers such as spins and cartwheels. Rodeo kayaking is a loosely organized competitive

The Olympic white-water competition is a thrilling test of speed and skill.

American Rebecca Giddens is one of the top-women kayakers in the world.

circuit that holds a world championship every two years. There you'll see some of the craziest and newest moves. Rodeo kayakers perform the **bow stall,** the **aerial backstab,** and the **roundhouse.**

Eric Jackson is arguably the strongest, most consistent rodeo kayaker in the world today. Jackson is always working on new moves. One of his recent creations is the McNasty. The McNasty is a full spin of the boat, while also making it stand on end. Jackson is a true innovator, and nobody is quite sure what he'll pull out of his bag of McTricks.

For Olympic Games medalist and U.S. national champion Rebecca Giddens, kayaking started out as a family activity.

Waterfall kayaking is an extreme version of the sport. Look out below!

ULTRA EXTREME: WATERFALL KAYAKING

Believe it or not, some people look for even bigger thrills from kayaking. Some have started going down waterfalls in kayaks. It's sort of like falling with style.

On August 23, 1999, Tao Berman launched himself and his kayak over a wickedly treacherous waterfall 98 feet 4 inches (30m) tall! According to *The Guinness Book of World Records,* that's the highest ever.

Because of crazy feats such as this one, Berman is regarded as the most extreme kayaker in the world today. But it's not just his hair-raising free fall that gains him such acclaim. Berman is also a world champion, a three-time world record holder, and a current member of the U.S. freestyle team.

The Giddens family learned to kayak at a YMCA camp, and as Rebecca excelled, she began entering competitions. Giddens was the U.S. Association of Canoe and Kayak's Female Athlete of the Year in 1999. She went on to win a silver medal in the 2002 Olympic Games. Giddens is one of the top-ranked women's slalom K-1 (single-paddler) competitors and a three-time national champion. She also has a 2002 world champion title to her name. Look for Rebecca Giddens to aim for gold at the 2004 Olympic Games.

Jackson and Giddens are at the very top of this fun sport. But there's plenty of room for the rest of us at the bottom. Kayaking is fun, easy to learn, and can take you to many new and wonderful places. See you on the water!

GLOSSARY

accessible—Able to be reached or achieved by a wide range of people.

aerial backstab—A move in which you spin on a wave and then let your bow rise, then "stab" the back of the boat into the water, stopping the spin.

beam—A long, thick piece of wood used to support the inside of a kayak.

blunt—Not sharp. Short and rounded.

bow stall—A whitewater move in which you paddle forward hard and bury the bow of your boat in the water so the back end pops up.

capsized—Turned over upside-down in the water.

chute—A tunnel in the whitewater that roars straight in one direction for a length of the river and descends downward.

eddies—Currents of water that flow in a different direction than the main current.

hole—A place in a river where water pours over a big rock or a river ledge; it can either be a fun place to play or very dangerous, sucking your boat in and over it; a crucial skill is learning to identify what type of a hole you've come upon.

hull—The main body of a boat. The bottom half.

Inuit—A person, or a group of people, from the Arctic north of Canada, Alaska, and Greenland. Inuits are also known as Eskimos.

maneuvers—Tricks or techniques.

roundhouse—An aggressive 180-degree spin on a wave against the grain. If you are carving over to your left, then you would spin, or *roundhouse,* to your right.

slalom—A race over a zigzag course past a series of poles or gates.

stabilize—Keep steady.

turbulent—Very wild and untamed, such as whitewater in a river.

FIND OUT MORE

On the Web

Visit our home page for lots of links about kayaking:
http://www.childsworld.com/links.html

NOTE TO PARENTS, TEACHERS, AND LIBRARIANS: We routinely check
our Web links to make sure they're safe, active sites—so encourage your
readers to check them out!

Books

Beazley, Bob, and Grant Tatum (illustrator). *Kayaking Essentials.*
Birmingham, Ala.: Menasha Ridge Press, 1995.

Johnson, Shelley. *The Complete Sea Kayaker's Handbook.* Camden,
Me.: Ragged Mountain Press/McGraw-Hill, 2002.

Stuhaug, Dennis O. *Kayaking Made Easy: A Manual for Beginners with Tips
for the Experienced.* Old Saybrook, Conn.: Globe Pequot Press, 1995.

INDEX

About the Author

Scott Bass is an avid outdoorsman who enjoys camping, fishing, and Hawaiian paddle surfing. He is the on-line editor, a staff writer, and a photographer for *Surfer* magazine and has written other books about action sports. Scott lives with his wife, Katrina, and their two children, Hank and Tessa, in Encinitas, California.

1068927498